3

COLORS, SHAPES, WORDS, AND NUMBERS

Alan Snow

Derrydale Books
New York

Colors

red
orange
yellow
green
blue
indigo
violet

Our world is full of colors. Just imagine if the sky wasn't blue or the grass wasn't green! Our world would be a very strange place. Here are a lot of different colors that you can see around you every day. How many colors can you name?

Did you know sunshine is made of many different colors? You can see all these colors in a rainbow. Rainbows appear when the sun shines on raindrops. The sunshine colors, that are normally all mixed up, become separate. There are seven colors in a rainbow.

black

white

violet

blue

green

yellow

orange

red

purple

Here are some colors you might find in a paint box. Which is your favorite color?

I asked these children to bring different colored objects to school. What did they bring?

Anyone want some juice?

This ink is a nice color.

What a lovely color!

I'm getting wet

Is it lunch time yet?

Do you like my pet frog?

Red mixed with blue makes purple.

We're mixing colors.

red

This room will look lovely when we're finished.

blue

purple

yellow

purple

red

blue

red

All the colors mixed together make brown.

orange

Watch the wet paint!

Red mixed with yellow makes orange.

What wet paint?

yellow

blue

green

green

green

Yellow mixed with blue makes green.

Color chart
This chart shows what happens when you mix colors. The bottom row of boxes shows what happens if you add white.

red	yellow	blue	red
orange		green	

| pink | light orange | yellow | light green | light blue | lilac | pink |

Shapes

The board is **square**.

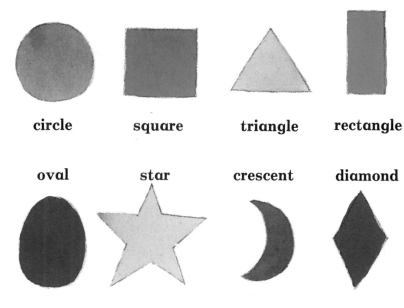

circle	square	triangle	rectangle
oval	star	crescent	diamond

Everything has a shape. Some shapes have names. Try to name some objects that are shaped like these shapes!

The kite is **diamond** shaped.

The wheels on this tricycle are **circles**.

The sails on the boat are **triangles**

*Look at all these **stars**.*

*Can you see the **crescent** moon?*

The egg is **oval** shaped.

This door is a **rectangle**.

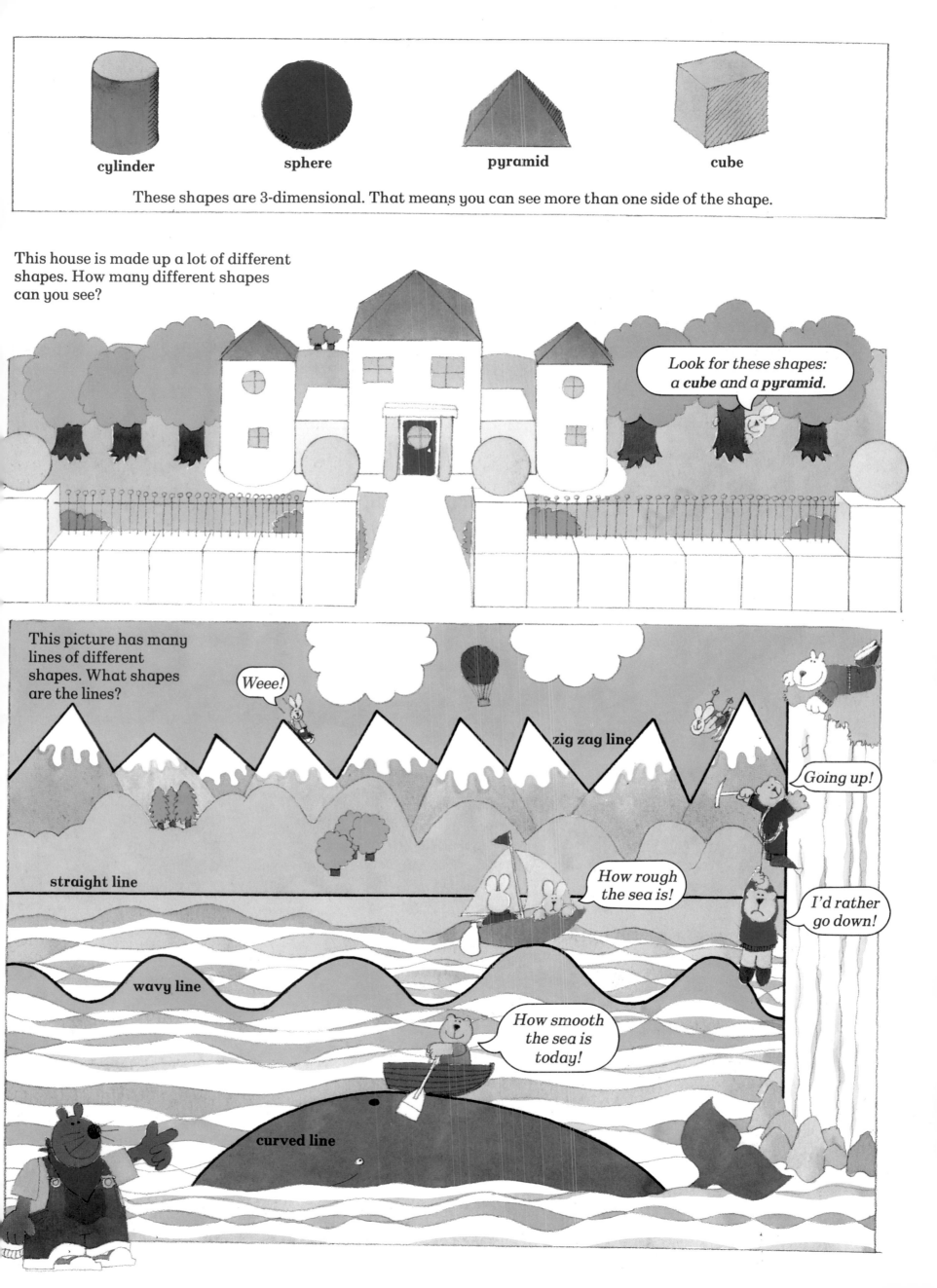

cylinder **sphere** **pyramid** **cube**

These shapes are 3-dimensional. That means you can see more than one side of the shape.

This house is made up a lot of different shapes. How many different shapes can you see?

Look for these shapes: a **cube** and a **pyramid**.

This picture has many lines of different shapes. What shapes are the lines?

Weee!

zig zag line

Going up!

straight line

How rough the sea is!

I'd rather go down!

wavy line

How smooth the sea is today!

curved line

Opposites

Activities

Look at all these busy people. What are they all doing? Do you know the words that tell us what they are doing?

Clothes

T-shirt **dress** **skirt** **sweater**

pants **overalls** **shirt**

underpants

undershirt **socks**

long johns

We need to wear clothes for all kinds of reasons; to keep cool, to keep warm, or to keep clean.

I'm getting dressed so I can go out and play!

When you get up in the morning, you dress for the day. When you go to bed at night, you put on your pajamas to sleep in.

If it is a hot day, I wear a hat to shade my head, a T-shirt and shorts so my arms and legs don't get too hot, and sandals to keep my toes cool.

When it rains I wear a hat to keep my head dry, a raincoat to keep my clothes from getting wet, and boots to keep my feet dry when I jump in all the puddles!

When it's very cold I wear a hat to keep my head warm, a scarf to keep my neck warm, a thick coat to keep the cold out, and boots to keep my feet warm.

My mom said I could choose my own clothes today. I'm very hot!

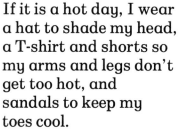

Numbers

It's fun to count! In this picture there are different objects all appearing in rows. Count the objects in each row. Then check the left side of the page to make sure you counted the right number.

Nice view!

1 — One sun

2 — Two hang gliders

3 — Three balloons

4 — Four airplanes

5 — Five

6
Six mountains

7
Seven trees

8
Eight houses

9
Nine cars

10
Ten friends

Big and Small

These cars are different sizes. One is small, one is big. How many cars are there altogether?

Many and Few

More and Less

Groups

How many groups of different musicians can you see in this big band? How many are in each group?

Addition

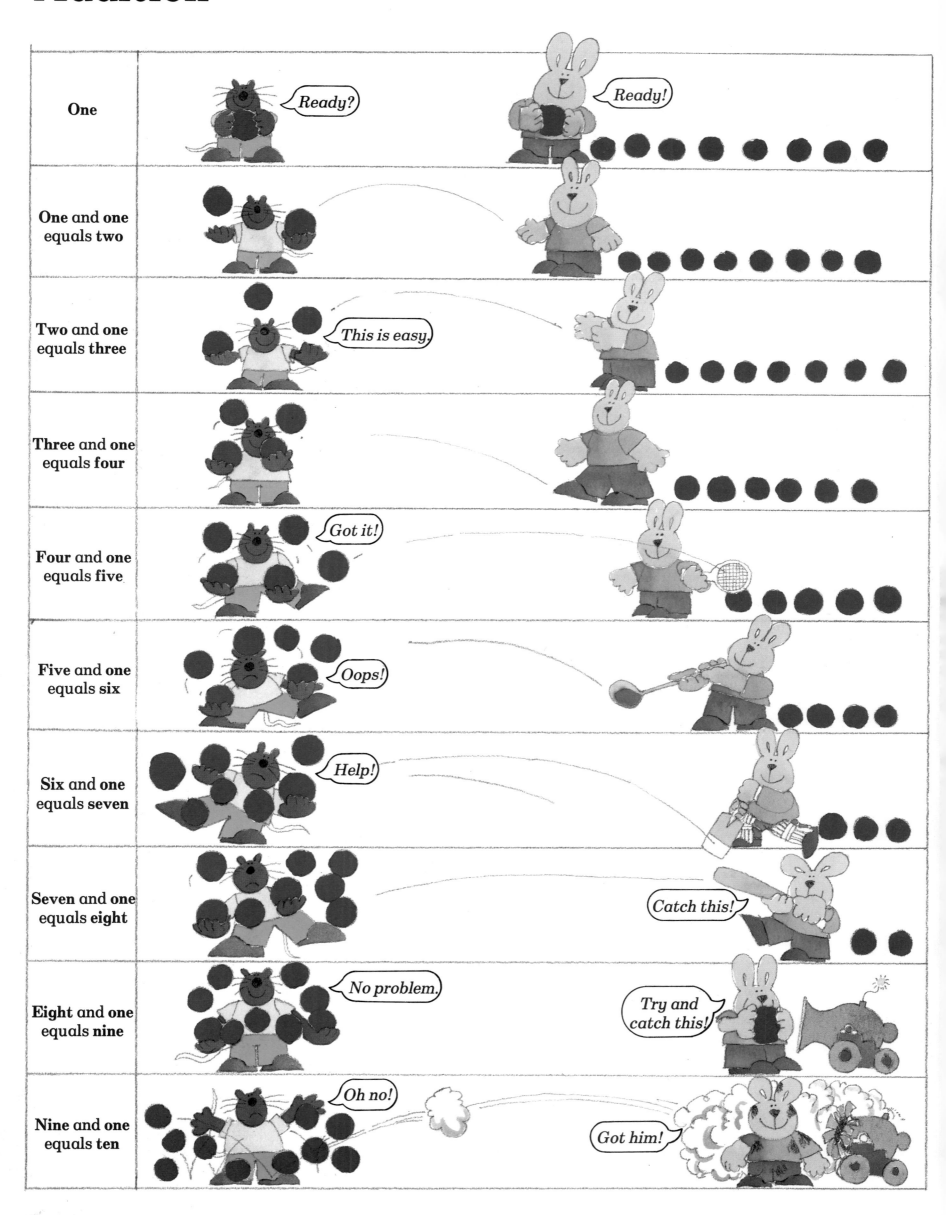

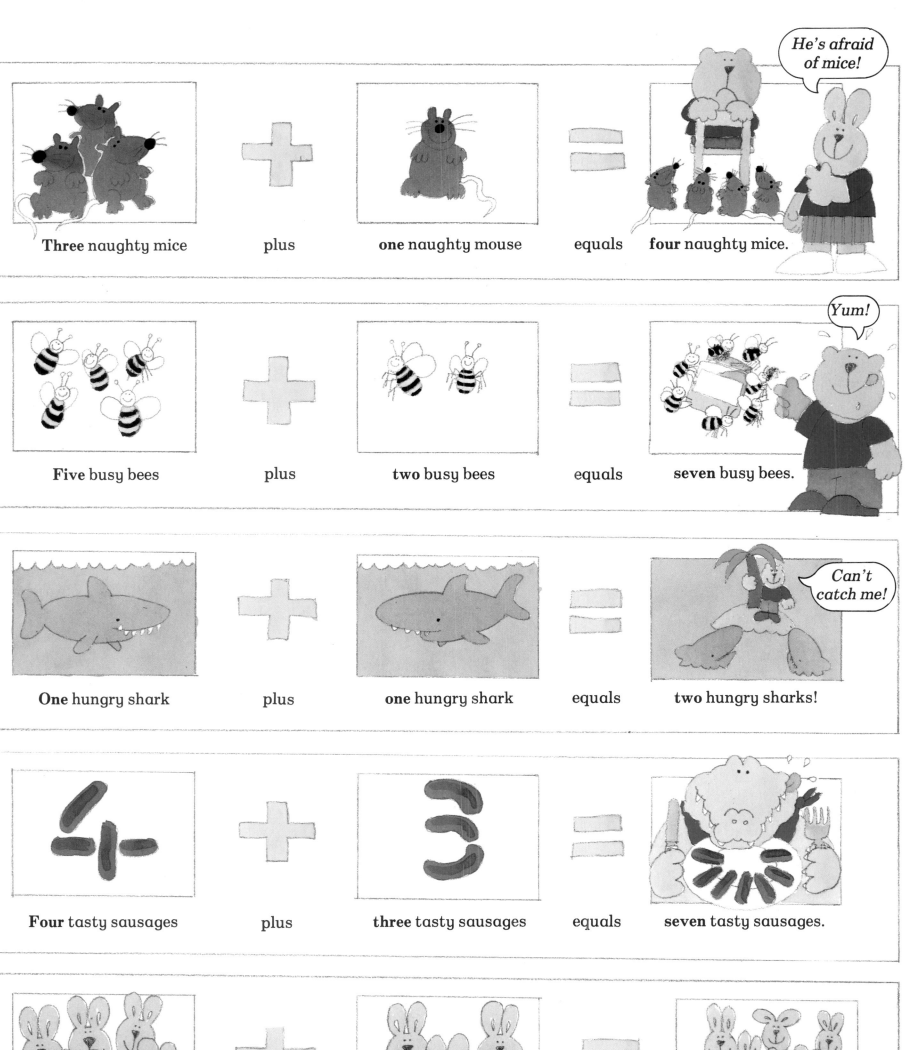

Three naughty mice   plus   **one** naughty mouse   equals   **four** naughty mice.

He's afraid of mice!

Five busy bees   plus   **two** busy bees   equals   **seven** busy bees.

Yum!

One hungry shark   plus   **one** hungry shark   equals   **two** hungry sharks!

Can't catch me!

Four tasty sausages   plus   **three** tasty sausages   equals   **seven** tasty sausages.

Five happy rabbits   plus   **three** happy rabbits   equals   **eight** happy rabbits.

Subtraction

There are **ten** apples. When the caterpillar has eaten **one**, there will be **nine** left.

Now there are **nine** apples. When the caterpillar has eaten another **one**, there will be **eight** left.

Now there are **eight** apples. When the caterpillar has eaten another **one**, there will be **seven** left.

Now there are **seven** apples. When the caterpillar has eaten another **one**, there will be **six** left.

Now there are **six** apples. When the caterpillar has eaten another **one**, there will be **five** left.

Now there are **five** apples. When the caterpillar has eaten another **one**, there will be **four** left.

Now there are **four** apples. When the caterpillar has eaten another **one**, there will be **three** left.

Now there are **three** apples. When the caterpillar eats another **one**, there will be **two** left.

Now there are **two** apples. When the caterpillar eats another **one**, there will be only **one** left.

There was **one** apple left, but someone else has eaten it, so there are **none** left.

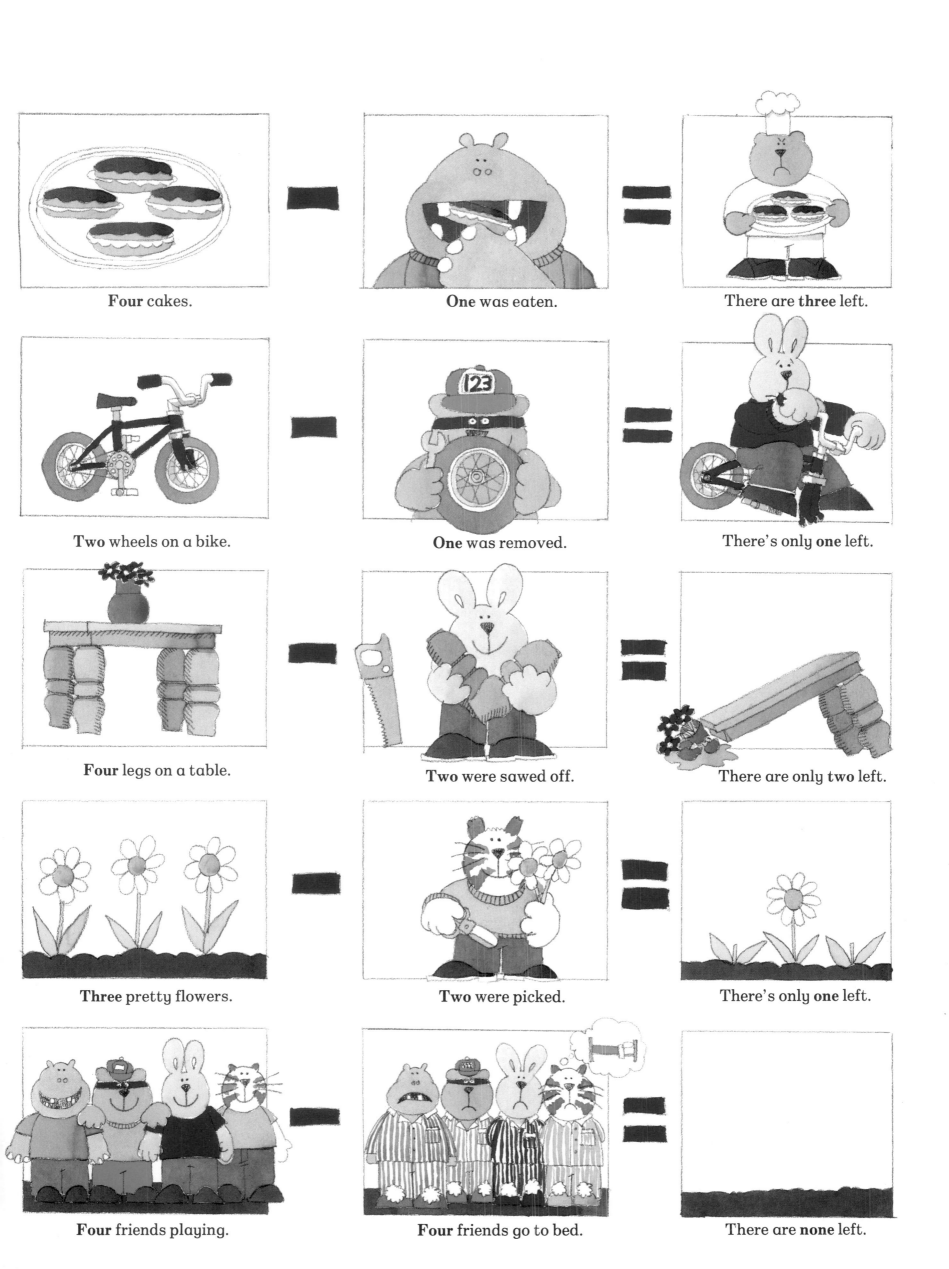

Four cakes.   **One** was eaten.   There are **three** left.

Two wheels on a bike.   **One** was removed.   There's only **one** left.

Four legs on a table.   **Two** were sawed off.   There are only **two** left.

Three pretty flowers.   **Two** were picked.   There's only **one** left.

Four friends playing.   **Four** friends go to bed.   There are **none** left.

You've seen how we add, and how we subtract. Can you find your own answers to these questions?

If there are **three** trees, and **one** is chopped down, how many are left?

I'm driving a bulldozer.

And I'm driving another bulldozer. How many bulldozers are there?

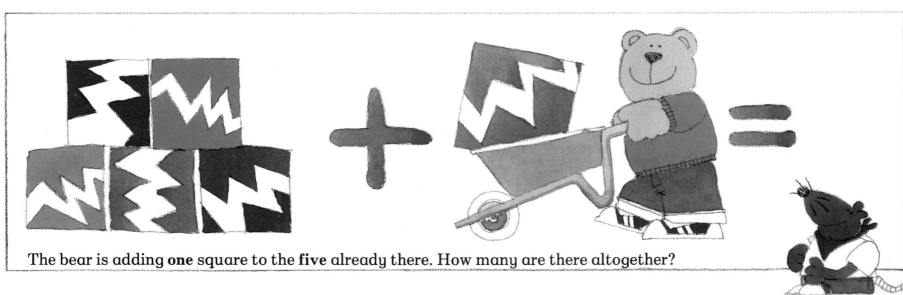

The bear is adding **one** square to the **five** already there. How many are there altogether?